HOW DID WE FIND OUT ABOUT
COMPUTERS?

The "HOW DID WE FIND OUT . . . ?" SERIES
by Isaac Asimov

HOW DID WE FIND OUT—
The Earth Is Round?
About Electricity?
About Numbers?
About Dinosaurs?
About Germs?
About Vitamins?
About Comets?
About Energy?
About Atoms?
About Nuclear Power?
About Outer Space?
About Earthquakes?
About Black Holes?
About Our Human Roots?
About Antarctica?
About Oil?
About Coal?
About Solar Power?
About Volcanoes?
About Life in the Deep Sea?
About the Beginning of Life?
About the Universe?
About Genes?
About Computers?
About Robots?
About the Atmosphere?
About DNA?
About the Speed of Light?

HOW DID WE FIND OUT ABOUT

COMPUTERS?

Isaac Asimov
Illustrated by David Wool

WALKER AND COMPANY
NEW YORK

First published in the United States of
America in 1984 by the Walker Publishing
Company, Inc.
Published simultaneously in Canada by
John Wiley & Sons Canada, Limited,
Rexdale, Ontario.
This edition printed in 1986.

Library of Congress Cataloging in Publication Data

Asimov, Isaac, 1920–
    How did we find out about computers?

    (The "How did we find out"—? series)
    Includes index.
    Summary: Traces the history of the computer, from the
ancient abacus through the mechanical calculating machine
to modern electronic technology.
    1. Computers—History—Juvenile literature.
[1. Computers—History] I. Wool, David, ill.   II. Title.
III. Series: Asimov, Isaac, 1920–   How did we find
out—series.
QA76.23.A85   1984   001.64   83-40401
ISBN 0-8027-6533-5 (lib. bdg.)

Printed in the United States of America

10 9 8 7 6 5 4 3

Contents

Dedicated to:
my brother-in-law,
John R. Jeppson,
the family expert in computers.

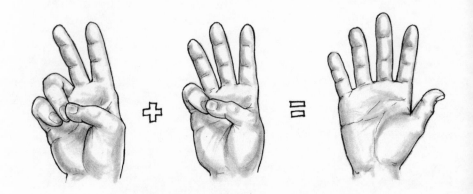

COMPUTING ON YOUR FINGERS

1 Abacuses and Slide Rules

WHEN WE FIRST started going to school, we learned to count and to write numbers: 1, 2, 3, 4, 5, 6, 7, 8, 9, 10, 11, 12, and so on.

Then we learned how to add and subtract numbers. We learned that $3+4=7$, that $5-4=1$, and so on. We were supposed to remember those additions and subtractions, but sometimes we didn't. What did we do when we forgot? Some of us would count on our fingers.

What is $3+4$? We would hold up three fingers, one after the other, counting: 1, 2, 3. Then we would hold up four more fingers: counting 1, 2—— and all the fingers on the hand would be used up. We would start on the other hand for the other two fingers: 3, 4. Then we would look at our hands. All the fingers on one hand would be held up and two fingers on the other. We would count all the fingers held up and there would be seven of them. That would tell us that $3+4=7$.

What is $5-4$? We would hold up five fingers one after the other, counting 1, 2, 3, 4, 5. We would next turn down four of those fingers, counting 1, 2, 3, 4. Only one finger would still be up, so $5 - 4 = 1$.

An expression used to describe the working out of additions, subtractions, and other ways of dealing with numbers is "to compute" (kom-PYOOT). This is another form of the expression "to count." In adding or subtracting you count, or compute, to get an answer. Anything that helps you compute can be called a "computer."

Of course, the original computer is your brain, because you can work out additions and subtractions in your head. Usually, though, the word is used for devices that help your brain get the answer. In that case, a person's fingers are the first computers.

One trouble is that you have only ten fingers. Suppose you want to solve $8 + 7$. You hold up eight fingers, counting them, and you then start to count off seven more fingers. However, once you've held up eight fingers, you only have two fingers left. What do you do?

You might take off your shoes and socks. Then, when you've counted off 1, 2, and used up all your fingers, you can begin on your toes: 3, 4, 5, 6, 7. You would then have counted all your fingers and five of your toes. That's fifteen altogether, so $8 + 7 = 15$.

It's troublesome to have to take off your shoes and socks to add numbers. Another way out is to ask a friend to hold up his fingers for you, but that can be troublesome, too. Your friend may not be around, or if he is, he may have other things to do.

A much better way is to hold up eight fingers, and then, if you want to add seven to that, you hold up two more fingers, 1, 2. Realizing that you have used up all your fingers, you write 10 on a piece of paper and start on your fingers all over, 3, 4, 5, 6, 7. You have five fingers up, and counting the ten you have written down (so as not to forget), you have 15 altogether.

But then why use fingers, when you only have ten? Why not use pebbles instead? Of course, you always have fingers with you, and you have to collect pebbles. Still, once you collect some pebbles you can put them in a little bag and always carry that around with you. You can collect as many as you wish; you can collect hundreds.

Making use of pebbles, you can add 254 and 127. First you count 254 pebbles and put them in one heap. Then you count out 127 pebbles and put them in another heap. You push the two heaps together and count them all. You find you have 381 pebbles, so $254 + 127 = 381$.

The Latin word for pebble is "calculus," so when we work out an arithmetic problem, we say we "calculate" (KAL-kyoo-late). "Calculate" and "compute" mean the same thing really, but nowadays we use "calculators" when we wish to speak of simple devices for helping us handle numbers. We use "computers" for more complicated devices.

Of course, it is tedious to count all those pebbles, so how about a short cut? Suppose you color the pebbles? A red pebble will mean 100, a white pebble will mean 10 and a blue pebble will mean 1. Therefore, for 254, you put two red pebbles, five white pebbles and four blue pebbles in one heap. For 127, you put one red pebble, two white pebbles and seven blue pebbles in another heap. The two heaps together contain three red pebbles, seven white pebbles and eleven blue pebbles. You can exchange ten of the blue pebbles (worth 1 each) for a white pebble (worth 10). That gives you three red pebbles, eight white pebbles and one blue pebble, so your answer is 381.

Even so, it is bothersome to carry pebbles around in a bag, and to have to remember which color is what, and then pick out the right colors to do the calculating.

Thousands of years ago, someone invented a wooden frame with wires across it. On each frame were strung ten little tiles that only filled up part of the wire, so they could be shoved back and forth.

All the tiles on the first wire are 1's; on the second wire, they are 10's; on the third wire they are 100's; on the fourth wire 1000's, and so on. You can go as high as you wish just by adding more wires.

In solving problems, you count the tiles on different wires, moving them from one side of the wire to the other. When ten tiles are moved, you move them back, and then move one tile on the next higher wire instead. Such a device is called an "abacus" (AB-uh-kus).

A person can quickly learn how to add and subtract on an abacus. It is very much like having a whole group of pairs of hands each with ten fingers. It would be even more like the different-colored pebbles, except that on the abacus all the tiles can be of the same color. They just have to be on different wires.

There are more complicated abacuses, where each wire has two compartments with five tiles in one and one or two tiles (worth 5 each, or 50, or 500) in the other. Abacuses can then be used for multiplication, division, and even more complicated operations.

The abacus must be worked entirely by hand. When you move all the tiles to one side on a particular wire, you must move them all back and push one tile on the

ABACUS

next wire instead. Is there any way of doing that automatically?

In 1644, a French mathematician, Blaise Pascal (pas-KAL, 1623-1662) built such a device. It consisted of a series of interlocking wheels. Each wheel could move through ten slots before making a complete turn, and with each slot, a number appeared in a small hole, starting with 0, then 1, 2, 3, 4, 5, 6, 7, 8, 9, and finally back to 0.

When it came back to 0, however, the wheel moved the next wheel to its left one notch forward. The wheel at the left changed from 0 to 1, so that if you added $9 + 1$, you got 10. Each time the wheel at the right made a full turn, the wheel to its left moved one more notch. Finally, you reached 99, and if you pushed the wheel at the right to the 0, the one to the left moved forward one notch to 0 and that pushed the wheel to *its* left to 1, so $99 + 1 = 100$. By pushing the wheels backward you could subtract.

Pascal's device was the first "mechanical calculator," the first device in which a human being didn't have to do all the work, but where the device itself did some of it.

Pascal's device could even multiply or divide. If you wanted the answer to 61×42, you just changed that to $61 + 61 + 61$—till you had added together forty-two 61's. You would get an answer of 2562.

That would take a long time, to be sure, and you could easily lose count. In 1671, a German mathematician, Gottfried Wilhelm Leibniz (LIBE-nitz, 1646-1716), worked out a device, more complicated than Pascal's, that could multiply and divide.

The mechanical calculators of Pascal and of Leibniz

BLAISE PASCAL (1623-1662)

BLAISE PASCAL'S MACHINE

never really came to be used in their time. They were expensive to make and they could only solve quite simple problems. It was easier to have human beings solve them on paper.

A device that became more popular started with a discovery by a Scottish mathematician, John Napier (NAY-pee-ur, 1550-1617). Between 1594 and 1614, he worked out a way of giving each number another number called a "logarithm" (LOG-uh-rith-um). Napier prepared tables in which you could look up the logarithm for any number you wanted.

Instead of multiplying two numbers, you looked up the logarithms of the two numbers and *added* them. The sum gave you a new logarithm, and if you looked up the number that fitted it, you would have the answer to the multiplication. Instead of dividing two numbers, you subtracted the logarithm of one from the logarithm of the other, and looked up the number that fitted the new logarithm.

Since it is easier to add and subtract than to multiply and divide, logarithms offered a very handy short-cut where complicated problems of multiplication and division were involved.

In 1632, an English mathematician, William Oughtred (AWT-red, 1574-1660), showed how to avoid wasting time looking up logarithms. He arranged numbers along a wooden ruler in such a way that the distance of each number from the starting point was equal to its logarithm. If two such rulers are put together and one is made to slide against the other, you can add the length of one number to the length of another. You would, in this way, add the logarithms and be able to read off the answer to a multiplication. If you slide one ruler against the other in the opposite direction, you subtract logarithms and read off the answer as a division.

Such devices are "slide rules". These became more elaborate so that you could solve more and more complicated problems quite quickly. As late as the 1960s, slide rules were necessary equipment for any scientist or student of science. I used one when I was in college, and I still own it today.

Until after World War II, abacuses, too, were much in use in countries such as Japan and China. In skilled hands, they could be as fast as slide rules.

Even Pascal's device didn't really die out. In cars, there is a little device that measures the total number of miles the car has traveled. It works exactly like Pascal's device.

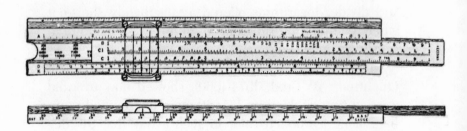

SLIDE RULE

2 Gears and Punch Cards

ONE TROUBLE WITH the slide rule is that it only gives approximate answers. I can solve $5,432 \times 4,739$ in a few seconds on the slide rule and get the answer 25,700,000. The real answer is 25,742,248. What's more, the slide rule doesn't tell me exactly how many places there are in the answer. The result might have been 2,570,000 or 257,000,000. I have to work out the correct number of places in my head.

The first person who tried to get exact-answer devices better than those worked out by Pascal and Leibniz was an English mathematician, Charles Babbage (BAB-ij, 1792-1871). He inherited money, and this allowed him to spend all his time on mathematical hobbies.

He was very careful about ways of calculating and it bothered him that logarithm tables (which are very complicated to work out) often had many errors that would give people wrong answers in their calculations. Babbage worked hard to find those errors and correct them.

CHARLES BABBAGE (1792-1871)

In 1822, he began to wonder if he might save himself a lot of trouble by building a machine that would calculate logarithms automatically for any number.

Babbage worked out the plans for a very complicated machine that would actually do the work. It consisted of many rods, wheels, ratchets and gears that would solve a whole series of arithmetical problems. Each solution would start a new problem that could be worked out for a new solution. Each solution would be nearer to the logarithm and eventually, there would be an answer close enough to the true logarithm to be put into the table.

Such a machine should never make a mistake—as long as all the rods, wheels, ratchets and gears were exactly the right size and shape, and fitted each other in exactly the right way.

But that was the catch. No matter how much money Babbage spent and how the workmen tried, the methods of the early 1800s weren't good enough to make all the parts of the machine exactly right. They didn't fit each other perfectly and would jam or slip, so that they would come up with wrong answers.

The more Babbage thought about it, however, the more enthusiastic he got. He decided that his logarithm-calculating machine wasn't enough. After all, it would just do that one job.

Why not devise a machine that could manipulate numbers in all sorts of ways so that it could be made to solve any kind of problem? It could be supplied with many kinds of rods, wheels, ratchets and gears, and it could then be switched from one combination to another in order to solve one kind of problem or another. Such a switch of combinations would be a way of in-

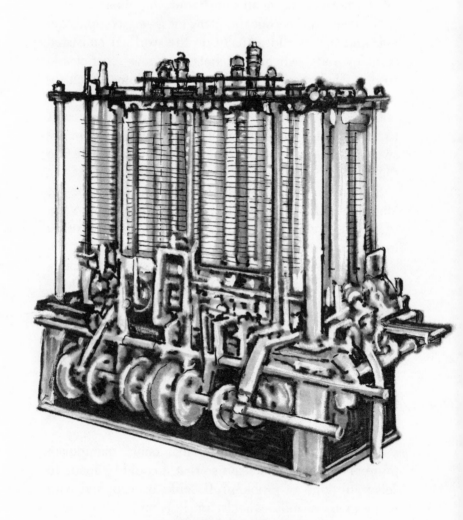

BABBAGE'S MACHINE

struction (or "programming") the device to solve a particular problem. The machine could ring a bell every time it finished some part of the problem.

Then, too, when the machine got a solution that it would have to use later on, it could hold the number by freezing a certain arrangement of rods, wheels and so on, until it was ready to use it. In this way, the machine had a "memory."

Finally, the machine could be attached to a printer so that the answer could be printed out.

A calculating device that is complicated enough to be programmed and to have a memory and a way of displaying an answer is what we call a "computer" today. The machine Babbage was trying to construct was the first computer.

Babbage was absolutely correct in his theories, but he simply never made all his parts fit together well enough for his device to work. He remained enthusiastic and kept getting more and more ideas so that he kept starting over in order to build something even *more* complicated, which made it even more certain that the necessary parts couldn't be made to fit. He managed to persuade the government and scientific societies to give him grants of money, and he not only used them up to no avail, he spent his entire private fortune on it, too.

He never did finish and his machine never did work. A piece of it still exists in the Science Museum in London.

People considered Babbage a failure and they thought he was simply a crank who dreamed up a wild machine that was only fit to be laughed at. They didn't stop to notice that his theory was actually correct, and eventually, most people forgot him.

He was born a century too soon. He needed things that no one had yet discovered in the early 1800s.

The way in which Babbage planned to control his machine dated back to the work of a French silk-weaver, Joseph-Marie Jacquard (zha-KAHR, 1752-1834).

In 1801, Jacquard had worked out a way of controlling the weaving loom so that a particular pattern could be worked out. The threads were carried by a series of rods. If some rods were allowed to work and some were held back, only certain threads would be woven into the fabric. If some rods worked at one time, and other rods at another time, the continuing change in threads could produce a pattern. Naturally, it took a human being to decide which rods were to be used at different times.

Or at least it did until Jacquard invented a system of stiff cards with holes punched in them. Some rods would be stopped by a card, but some would pass through the holes. By using different kinds of punched cards that moved into place automatically, one after the other, different sets of rods would do their work in such a way that a pattern would be worked into the fabric without human beings having to do a thing. This is the "Jacquard loom."

Babbage used punch cards to control the workings of his device but, as I explained, nothing came of it. Fifty years later, however, punch cards were used in a device that *did* work.

It happened in the United States. Throughout the 1800s, the United States was increasing in population, size, and wealth. Every ten years, the federal govern-

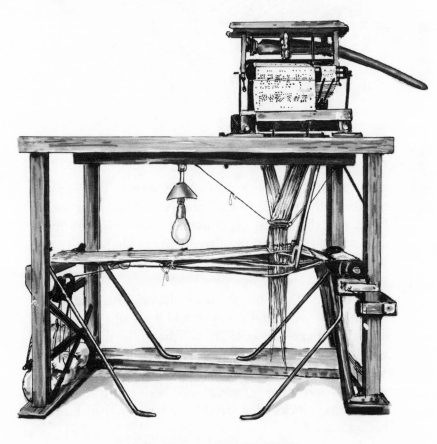

JACQUARD'S FIRST LOOM

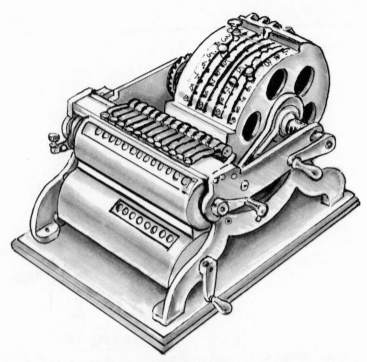

CALCULATOR BUILT IN 1875

ment must conduct a census (SEN-sus). The census counts all the people in the country and finds out about their age, their jobs, their homes, and how they live. This was very important in trying to decide how to continue to develop the United States and make it richer still.

In the 1880 census, so much material was gathered that it took years and years to add it all up, work it all out, and make sense of it. By the time the job was nearly finished it was almost time for the 1890 census. Some way had to be found to work more quickly with numbers and other information. There had to be some mechanical device that would work faster than human beings could.

By the 1880s, there had been important advances. Wheels and gears and such items could be manufactured in smaller sizes and with greater accuracy. They could fit together better.

Machines could therefore be built along the lines of Pascal and Leibniz that would work well and wouldn't be too large or too expensive. A number of these were manufactured and sold to various offices.

They could even be made to do rather complicated work. In the 1870s, for instance, a British scientist, William Thomson, who was later made Lord Kelvin (1824-1907), worked out such a device. It had cleverly adjusted gears and wheels that allowed the machine to calculate the times of high and low tide at a given place on the seashore. It could do so for years into the future.

It did this in a special way. Most calculating machines handle numbers. These are "digital calculators" (DIJ-ih-tal) or, if they are complicated enough, "digital computers." (The word "digit" means both "a number" and "a finger or toe," which shows how people once used fingers and toes to work with numbers.) Babbage's machine was intended to be a digital computer.

Some calculating machines don't deal with numbers, but with other things that match numbers or are "analogous" to them. They are "analog calculators" (AN-uh-log) or "analog computers." A slide rule measures lengths along the ruler, and it is an analog calculator. Kelvin's machine measured the distance through which gears turned and it was an analog calculator, too. (The future, however, lay with digital devices.)

In addition to the manufacture of improved parts, electricity was coming into use,* and it could be made to do some of the work.

*See *How Did We Find Out About Electricity?* (1973)

THE HOLLERITH TABULATOR

During the 1880s, an American inventor, Herman Hollerith (HOL-uh-rith, 1860-1929), tackled the problem of the census. He made use of punch cards as Jacquard and Babbage did. Every card could be punched according to the data gathered in the census. Holes in particular places could mean that a person was male or female, in his sixties or in his forties, a farmer or a factory worker, and many other things.

In order to add up and analyze all this information, the cards were placed on a stand and a metal device was pressed down against it. The device had many pins, which would be stopped by the cardboard. Wherever there was a hole, however, a pin would go through and reach a pool of mercury underneath. Electricity would pass through that pin and control the pointer on a particular dial. People didn't have to count or add. As the punch cards were sent rapidly through the machine, people just recorded the numbers indicated on the dials.

The 1890 census was handled by the Hollerith punch card system. Even though the amount of information gathered in the 1890 census was much greater than that of the 1880 census, the 1890 census was completely analyzed in only one-third the time of the earlier one.

For the first time, human beings were presented not with a mechanical calculating device, but an "electromechanical" one.

In 1896, Hollerith founded a company devoted to making all kinds of machines that could handle and analyze information. He called it the "Tabulating Machine Company." It grew and grew and eventually adopted the name of "International Business Machines Corporation." This is now usually known by its initials as "IBM."

**VANNEVAR BUSH'S DIFFERENTIAL ANALYZER
(MIT—1930)**

3 Binary Numbers and Switches

EVEN THE MOST successful calculating machines of the 1800s did not match Babbage's dream. The ones that worked were all designed to solve one kind of problem. Hollerith's machine could only work with problems similar to the census. Kelvin's machine could only work for tides, and so on.

In 1876, however, Kelvin wrote a paper showing that machines could be programmed for all kinds of problems. He had revived Babbage's idea of half a century before—that of an all-purpose computer.

However, people realized how large and complicated such a machine would have to be, so no one tried to build one for another half-century.

The person who finally tackled the job was an American engineer, Vannevar Bush (1890-1974).

In 1925, he began to build what he called a "differential analyzer." It could be used to solve any kind of problem that included certain complicated mathematical relationships called "differential equations." It took five years to build the machine, and it proved to be a very large device. It was so large it had to be run by electric motors rather than by hand. (There were no electric motors in Babbage's time, of course).

Most of it was mechanical, just as Babbage's machine had been, though, of course, the mechanical parts were far better made. Bush realized, however, that good as the parts might be, the machine wouldn't work well if it were entirely mechanical. He therefore made use of something new.

Scientists had learned how to force an electric current through a "vacuum" (VAK-yoo-um)—a space in which nothing existed, not even air. The current passing through consisted of a stream of tiny electrically charged particles called "electrons" (ee-LEK-tronz). This electron stream could be easily stopped and started. It could be made to control the activity of parts of the machine just as Holerith's punch cards could.

Bush made use of glass bulbs with vacuums inside and with metal devices for starting and stopping the electron stream. In the United States these are usually called "tubes." (They are often called "radio tubes" because they were most frequently used in radios.) Bush put these tubes in certain places where they could be used to stop and start an electric current, so that they acted as "switches." Because streams of electrons were involved, Bush's machine was partly "electronic."

Bush's machine was the first ever to be built and *made to work* that could be programmed, that had a memory, and so on. It was the first device that could be called a *computer* in the present meaning of the word. Sixty years after his death, Babbage's dream had finally come true.

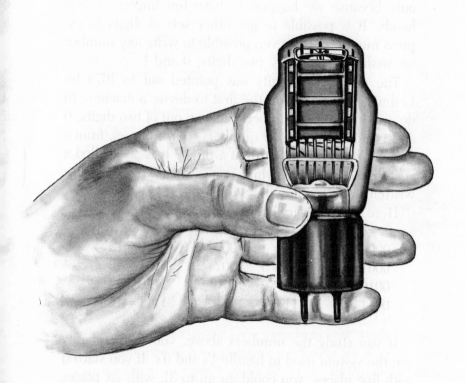

VACUUM TUBE

Once Bush's differential analyzer was completed in 1930, other scientists became very interested in the matter of solving problems by machines. In doing so, they tried to apply mathematical discoveries of the past to such machines.

For instance, we make use of ten different digits in writing numbers: 0, 1, 2, 3, 4, 5, 6, 7, 8, and 9. That is only because we happen to have ten fingers on our hands. It is possible to use other sets of digits to express numbers. It is even possible to write any number we wish by using only two digits, 0 and 1.

The use of two digits was pointed out in 1679 by Leibniz, who had been the first to devise a machine to do multiplication. Numbers built up out of two digits, 0 and 1, are called "binary numbers" (BY-nuh-ree), from a Greek word meaning "two at a time." It is also called a "two-based system," while our ordinary numbers are written in a "ten-based system."

Here's how binary numbers work:

$0000 = 0$	$0100 = 4$	$1000 = 8$	$1100 = 12$
$0001 = 1$	$0101 = 5$	$1001 = 9$	$1101 = 13$
$0010 = 2$	$0110 = 6$	$1010 = 10$	$1110 = 14$
$0011 = 3$	$0111 = 7$	$1011 = 11$	$1111 = 15$

If you study the numbers above, you will probably see the system used to handle 1's and 0's. If you started with five places, you could go up to 31; with six places up to 63; and so on. If you use enough places, you can use a series of 1's and 0's to represent millions and billions of numbers. Each number would have a particular series. If you were given any particular series, you could figure out what number it is in the ordinary ten-based system.

Even if you don't see exactly how the binary numbers work, that isn't important now. You just have to understand that two digits can be used to write any number.

It didn't occur to anyone, at first, that binary numbers would be particularly important to calculating machines. It seemed natural to use wheels marked off with all ten digits, as Pascal did.

Once tubes began to be used in computers, though, people were controlling electron streams, starting and stopping them. Every time a tube lets the stream pass, that can represent the digit "1"; every time it stops the stream, that can represent the digit "0".

That means it is possible to represent numbers by electron streams going "on" and "off." The streams can go on and off much faster than gears can make wheels turn, and the streams won't jam or slip the way gears and wheels might. In that way, a device using tubes could do anything that one using gears could do, and would be faster and more reliable as well.

Then, in 1854, an English mathematician named George Boole (1815-1864) worked out a way of dealing with "logic." (Logic is the name given to the way people reason when they are trying to work out any kind of problem, even one that is not mathematical.) Boole worked out a way of representing logical statements in symbols instead of in ordinary English words. He showed how to manipulate the symbols so as to come out with an answer. In a way, he made logic into a kind of mathematics, and his system was called "symbolic logic."

In 1913, symbolic logic was improved and brought even closer to mathematics by two English mathematicians, Alfred North Whitehead (1861-1947) and Bertrand A. W. Russell (1872-1970).

In the 1940s, an American mathematician, Claude Elwood Shannon (1916-) began to work out a system whereby methods of turning electron streams on and off would not only represent numbers, but also the symbols of symbolic logic. When he finally got his notions all worked out by 1949, he called it "information theory" because it showed how to handle information of all kinds.

This was the first important advance beyond Babbage's theories and showed how machines could be designed to solve any non-mathematical problem that could be put into symbolic logic.

While Shannon was working on his theory, people were trying to build machines that would calculate by using on-off switches that represented binary numbers. They were doing so in Germany, in the United States, and in Great Britain.

In Germany, an engineer named Konrad Zuse (T ZOO-zuh, 1910-), built a machine using binary numbers in 1936. It was eventually called "Z-1." The switches he used were "electromagnetic relays." Such a switch can be pulled shut by a magnetic pull so that a current will run, or it can be allowed to open when the magnetism is stopped so that the current is stopped, too. When the magnet is on it's a "1," when it's off it's a "0."

In a few years, Zuse decided that if he used tubes instead of relays, the electron stream could be handled more neatly and quickly than an electric current

AIKEN'S MARK ONE (1943)

through a wire. It would be better, he felt, to have electronic switches than ordinary electrical ones.

But then, in 1939, World War II began. Germany, under the fascist dictator Adolf Hitler (1889-1945), began to win victory after victory. Hitler was interested in new scientific advances, but only those that could be developed quickly since he thought the war would soon be won. He wasn't interested in computers, so Zuse got no financial support.

Meanwhile, in the United States an American mathematician at Harvard, Howard Hathaway Aiken (AY-ken, 1900-1973) was working along the same lines, although he had no knowledge of what Zuse was doing. Aiken managed to get financial backing from Hollerith's old company, which was now IBM, so he was luckier than Zuse in that way.

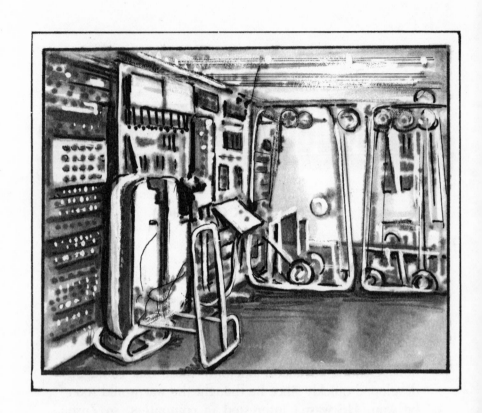

COLOSSUS—DESIGNED TO BREAK CODES

When the United States entered the war in 1941, Aiken joined the Navy. The American government, however, realized how hard it was for a ship to solve the problem of aiming a huge gun correctly in order to hit another ship that might be a mile or more away. (Each ship is moving, and the direction and speed of the wind has an effect, and so on. By the time all the calculations were made in the ordinary way, everything was changed and the calculations would have to be made all over again.) Aiken was given leave, therefore, to work on his device. He wasn't neglected, as Zuse was.

Aiken, like Zuse, used electromagnetic relays, but he did not even try to use tubes. He felt that tubes might be faster but they were also less reliable. In 1943, he had the machine, eventually called "Mark I," finished.

Meanwhile, Great Britain was also interested in working out a calculating device. Their reason for wanting to do so was to be able to work out the complicated German codes that were used for transmitting secret messages. If machines could be devised that could try out enormous numbers of possibilities very quickly, until something was found that made sense, a code could be broken. Germany would then be sending messages she thought were secret, while Great Britain would be able to read them at once, and be prepared in advance for whatever Germany was planning to do.

Then, too, Great Britain could use its device to work out a code that could not be broken by Germany unless it had an equally good calculating machine.

Guided mostly by a mathematician, Alan Mathison Turing (1912-1954), the British worked out a machine for the purpose. It was called "Colossus" and it was in operation at the close of 1943. By the end of the war, ten such machines had been built.

Colossus was different from Z-1 and Mark I in that it used tubes as switches, two thousand of them. It was the first all-electronic calculating device, but it was only useful for a special purpose—breaking codes. The British felt Germany might not have been defeated were it not for Colossus, so it's a good thing that Hitler had never been interested in supporting Zuse.

4 Tubes and Transistors

THESE EARLY MACHINES, then, were either general purpose, but not electronic; or electronic, but not general purpose. What was needed was an all-electronic general-purpose device, something that could be considered an "electronic computer."

In 1944, an American engineer at the University of Pennsylvania, John William Mauchly (MAWCH-lee, 1907-1980), decided to build such a machine. In partnership with a younger engineer, John Presper Eckert, Jr. (1919-), he got to work.

The two knew nothing of Colossus, which the British had built in the strictest secrecy, so they didn't have that to go by, but they succeeded anyway. When they finally completed it in 1946, it had 18,000 tubes in it. It did not use binary numbers, though, but ordinary ten-based ones.

Mauchly and Eckert called it the "Electronic Numerical Integrator and Calculator," or ENIAC, for short.

ENIAC was the world's first electronic computer. It was shown to the public in 1946 and, even though the

ENIAC (1946)

use of ten-based numbers slowed it down, it could do very complicated arithmetic in a fraction of a second.

At last, the human being was definitely outclassed in arithmetic. As late as 1946, a skillful person with an abacus could solve problems faster than people using calculators. ENIAC, however, could handle numbers a thousand or more times as fast as a man at an abacus could. Once ENIAC was programmed, it was only necessary to push a button.

For the first time, people were aware of what had been accomplished by all the people from Pascal onward. They began to talk about "electronic brains."

ENIAC was just *barely* all-purpose, however. It could be programmed and switched from one kind of calculation to another, but only with a great deal of trouble.

But then a Hungarian-American mathematician, John von Neumann (NOY-mahn, 1903-1957), got the idea of storing the programs inside the computer's memory. In that case, it would no longer be necessary to reprogram a computer with a lot of complicated fiddling every time you wanted it to do something new. You would just switch it from one program to another at the touch of a button.

Mauchly and Eckert went on to build computers that were simpler and better than ENIAC. In 1951, they had UNIVAC ("Universal Automatic Computer") which was the first computer to be sold commercially.

There was still an important problem to be solved. The tubes were unreliable, just as Aiken had insisted. They were made of glass and could break. Even if they didn't, they would gradually grow leaky so that the vacuum inside would be spoiled. For that reason, tubes were always breaking down and having to be replaced.

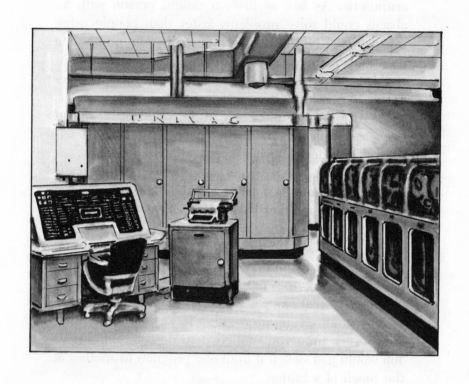

UNIVAC (1951)

Then, too, tubes were rather large. There had to be enough vacuum inside to keep the stream of electrons from flowing unless they were forced to do so. If you had tens of thousands of large tubes, the computer ended up being *very* large.

Another problem was that in order to force the electrons to flow, the devices inside the tubes had to be heated to extremely high temperatures. That took a lot of energy, and when you had many, many tubes, they had to be spaced far apart in order not to heat each other so much that the entire computer broke down. That meant the computer had to be larger still, and all the energy that had to be used made the computer very expensive, too. What's more, it took time for the tubes to grow hot and that slowed things up.

There didn't seem to be anything you could do about all of this, and it might have seemed to some that computers would forever be huge and expensive and would always be pretty unreliable.

In 1948, however, an English-American scientist, William Bradford Shockley (1910-), along with two American co-workers, Walter Houser Brattain (1902-) and John Bardeen (1908-), discovered a substitute for the tube.

Certain solid materials—for instance, "silicon" (SIL-ih-kon), a common substance that can be obtained from any rocky material—could be set up in such a way that electrons could drift through them. These "solid-state devices" could be used to control the drifting electrons in just the same way a tube can control a stream of electrons. A solid-state device that could do everything a tube could do came to be called a "transistor" (tran-SIS-ter).

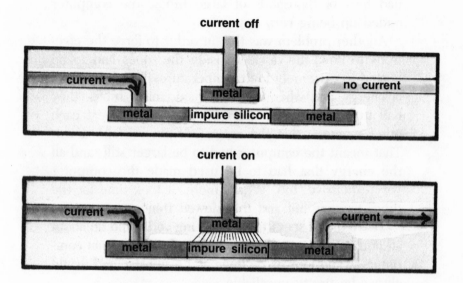

current off

current

no current

metal

metal

impure silicon

metal

current on

current

current

metal

metal

impure silicon

metal

HOW A TRANSISTOR WORKS

The transistor had many advantages over the tube. It was solid and sturdy so that it would neither break nor leak. It did not involve a sizable amount of vacuum, so that a transistor could be much smaller than a tube and still do its work. It didn't take any heat to start a transistor working, so that it used up almost no energy and it started immediately.

Of course, when transistors were first developed, they were pretty unreliable, because scientists didn't know how to design them so that they would work well. They soon learned to make them work better and more reliably, however, while also finding ways to make them smaller and cheaper.

TWO TRANSISTORS ON A SILICON CHIP

The invention of the transistor was the great turning point in the history of the computer. As long as there were only gears and wheels, computers couldn't be built at all. Once there were electrical relays and electronic tubes, computers could be built, but they had to be fearfully large and expensive.

With transistors, it became possible to make them smaller and cheaper. In fact, once computers came to be "transistorized," they also came to be "miniaturized."

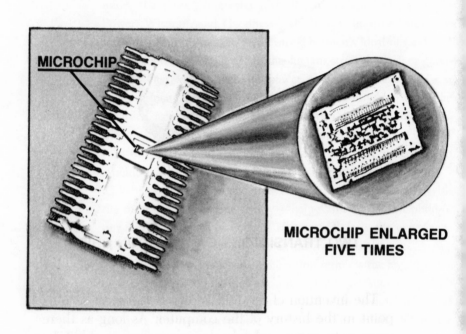

MICROCHIP

**MICROCHIP ENLARGED
FIVE TIMES**

5 Chips and Microchips

AT FIRST, MINIATURIZATION only went so far. Computers were still made as they were before, except that every time it would have been necessary to put in a tube, a transistor was put in instead, and that was much smaller. What's more, transistors could be crowded much more closely together than could tubes.

That resulted in a considerable miniaturization, but transistors weren't all there was to a computer. Each transistor had to be connected to many other parts. The transistor plus the other parts made up a "circuit," a passageway through which the electric current traveled. The transistors were the switches that turned the current on and off, but they weren't the entire circuit by any means.

For this reason, although computers got smaller, they were still held up by the size of the circuits, and this kept them from getting smaller still.

But then, in the 1960s, scientists began to learn how to miniaturize the whole circuit.

They started with small, thin squares of pure silicon,

POCKET CALCULATOR

and then added tiny traces of certain other substances to it. The surface could be carved into tiny parts, each of which behaved like a different part of a circuit. The different parts would be connected with tiny strips of metal so that an "integrated circuit" was achieved—an entire circuit on a single "chip" of silicon.

Little by little, scientists learned how to make the chips smaller so that the "microchip" came into being. And they learned how to squeeze more and more circuits on them, until they were forced to manufacture such devices under a microscope.

Eventually, they could make computers very small indeed and yet have them capable of doing far more than ENIAC could possibly have done, and far more quickly, too. And of course, they cost much less.

For a few dollars, you can now buy pocket calculators that can add, subtract, multiply, divide and do many other things in split-seconds and that take almost no energy to run.

I have one such pocket calculator with special "photoelectric cells" built into it, cells which form tiny amounts of electricity when exposed to light.* Enough electricity is formed if the pocket calculator is put under the light of an ordinary desk lamp to keep it running. It never has to be plugged in anywhere, nor does it ever have to have battery replacements.

I also have an electronic computer that is scarcely any larger and that can be programmed to do tasks far more easily, and do them far better and faster than all of ENIAC could have done forty years ago, even

*See *How Did We Find Out About Solar Power?* (1981)

though ENIAC filled a large room and took a vast amount of energy to run, while my own computer fits into my jacket pocket.

To summarize——

In the 1950s, the American government started using computers to do the necessary calculations that would keep track of tax collections, deal with the very complicated work on nuclear weapons, and help us in the space race with the Soviets. It took whole governments to be able to afford computers.

In the 1960s, large industries began to use computers, which were now smaller, cheaper, and better. They used them to keep track of their accounts, of what they sold and bought, and of all their complicated bookkeeping.

In the 1970s, computers were even smaller, cheaper, and better. They worked their way into every office. Banks kept track of each deposit, each check, each withdrawal. Other businesses used them to organize their payrolls.

Now, in the 1980s, computers are still smaller, cheaper and better than before and are beginning to come into every home. Therefore, we now speak of the "home computer."

Computer games are the most popular form of home computer right now. In those games, tiny objects appear on a television screen, following complicated maneuvers that are guided by the programming of the computer. A person playing the video game can control the motion of certain objects by adjusting a lever, or similar form of controlling device. The player tries to outmaneuver the computer program, to destroy "enemy ships" for instance, before he is himself destroyed.

COMPUTER GAME PLUGGED INTO TV SET

Most of the video games take on the appearance of war or violent adventure because that is exciting, but it is also possible to play more intellectual games. A home computer can be programmed to play chess, and a human player can then try to beat the computer. Some chess programs are so good that computers using them can beat all but very good human players. The time may soon come when the world chess champion is a computer!

Home computers can also do work. This book, for instance, is now being written on a word processor.

The words I type appear on a television screen. After I have typed a page, I can stop to look at it, and retype some words or whole paragraphs. I can eliminate a word here and there, or a whole sentence or paragraph, by pushing certain keys on the board. I can add a word here and there, or a whole sentence or paragraph, by pushing other keys. I can switch the order of paragraphs, renumber pages, search out particular words all through a manuscript, highlight any words that are misspelled.

In other words, I can "edit" the manuscript right on the screen by giving the word processor the proper instructions.

Whatever I do leaves no marks. When I am finished, the manuscript on the television screen looks fresh and clean.

I can then (if I wish) have all the pages I have written printed automatically on paper just as though they were being typewritten, except that the typewriting is done four times as fast as I can possibly type. What's more, it takes place without any errors, provided that I have not carelessly left any errors on the television screen.

ISAAC ASIMOV AT HIS WORD PROCESSOR

The programming for such an operation is on a thin plastic disc that looks like a small phonograph record that is flexible and can bend. It is usually called a "floppy disc." All the words on the screen are recorded on the floppy disc. One of my floppy discs will hold 125 typewritten pages, or four books the size of this one.

If I don't want to take the trouble to have my manuscript printed out, I can send the floppy discs themselves to the publisher and, if he has the equipment, he can have it appear on his television screen and do further editing. Or he can have it printed in book form directly.

Someday soon, every home may be connected to remote computers that contain many kinds of day-to-day information.

It will then be possible, by punching the proper directions into a keyboard in your living room, to find out what the weather is going to be like tomorrow, or what the latest news headlines are, or how the stock market is doing, or what the baseball scores are, or what the bargains for the day are at the supermarket or department store, and so on.

In fact, all the information in all the libraries in the world might be placed into computers, so that by asking the right questions you can get any information you need. You could get lists of books on any subjects. You could arrange to have the pages of any particular book displayed. You could have the computer show you any paragraphs in that book that deal with a particular subject. You could have any material printed out that you might want to keep for a while.

When this happens, a computer becomes a "teaching machine." Anyone, whether a child or a grown-up, can begin to educate himself or herself by asking the computer the right questions, and learning what is displayed by it.

Thinking of all this, we must ask ourselves whether the time will ever come when computers become "smarter" than human beings. Will they someday be able to do anything a human being can do, and more, too? Will they actually replace human beings?

Perhaps not.

The human brain is made up of about 10,000,000,000 "neurons" (NYOO-ronz), or "nerve cells,"each of which is connected with many others.

No computer has that many components as yet, and even if it had, the neuron is not just a switch, the way a transistor is; or a simple pathway, as a circuit is. Each neuron is made up of many billions of complicated molecules, so that even a single neuron is more complicated than any computer we have yet built.

There are some things a computer can already do far better than the human brain can. Even Hollerith's punch-card machine, a hundred years ago, could do certain arithmetical tasks far more quickly than human brains could, and with far less chance of error.

However, human brains possess such things as intuition, insight, imagination, fantasy, and creativity, which computers don't yet have. What's more, we don't know how to program computers for such things because we don't understand the way in which we ourselves possess and make use of such talents.

For example, when I write a story, I write as fast as I can and put one word after another in just the right order until I am finished.

But how can I tell a computer to do it? Even if I put

a whole dictionary of words into its memory, how can I tell it what word to put first, and what second, and what third? How can I explain to it how to choose the order of words so that it can write a brand-new story, just the way I do it, when I don't know how I do it?

Perhaps some day, we will learn how to program a computer to do this, but it will very likely be such a complicated program and so enormous a task that there would be no sense in trying to design a computer of that sort. Human beings could do it so much more easily themselves.

Instead we will end up having two varieties of intelligence: computer and human. Each will do the tasks it is best at, and the two will cooperate. In cooperation they will be able to do far more than either type of intelligence would be able to do alone.

Think of what kind of future we might have; what wonderful tasks computers and human beings might accomplish in cooperation.

The day might come when human beings will look back with horror to the days before they had computers as friends and helpers in the task of solving the problems of the universe.

And if, by then, computers can think well enough, they will be thankful, too, that human beings exist to do the marvellous guessing and imagining that they themselves cannot do.

Index